IN THE DETAILS

THOMAS HINDS

SECOND EDITION

This book is dedicated to my high school teacher, Patty Rhoderick,
who taught my Senior English class.

Without your encouragement and help, I might have put the idea of
my words being worth remembering into a dark closet where they
never would have seen the light of day. Thank you so much for your
friendship. It means more to me than you may ever know. Teachers
like you give hope and vision to the future of the next generation.

Much love to you forever and always.

IN THE DETAILS

She wants smeared lipstick,
Buttons torn from her blouse,
Goosebumps and bitemarks
And JBF hair.

She wants half-dazed mornings,
Coffee-stained smiles,
And the good kind of sore.

She wants passion,
Strobe lights
Flashing in brilliance,
Crackling firelight,
Breathless moments,
Dilating pupils,
And bedroom in disarray.

Mostly, she wants to taste life,
Live outside grey lines,
Paint with the colors of her dreams,
And embrace every part of herself.

She wants to share all this with you;
Don't take her desire for granted.
She has bottled these dreams up for years,
Yet you fail to notice.

Count your blessings,
Then help her fill in the details
With the beauty of her life's novel.

CONTENTS

I. FINITE

FLAWED BEAUTY

I did not fall in love

With the chance of perfection.

It was her flawed beauty

That fed my hunger,

My desire to kiss every scar,

Soothe every battle wound.

Beneath gray blue skies

I closed my eyes,

Trying to remember how to breathe.

The tattoo she hid,

Black and blue like our love;

I am her melancholy.

She found a way to share her shattering

In the darkness, in these arms.

As the sun rose,

Her mask appeared

As she slipped

Into the light of a new day.

She tried to hide

Behind locked doors

With broken keys and closed shutters.

Inside the isolation,

She raged against the storm

Torrents within her own mind.

She prayed for someone
To kick in her doors,
Sweep away the gray,
And let her bathe in the warm sun.
She knew she was lost
In her own darkness.

But in the cobwebbed corner,
She saved a sliver of hope.

TANGLE

The music inside his head
Was a tangle—
A symphony of chaos,
A mangled love song.

How could he be expected to sing
When the melody
Escaped like a sigh in a hurricane?

He despised his wretched hands
Penning notes and phrases
Silent to the outside world,
Yet blistering to his ears.

He grasped at rusty rings.
Lost in a momentary blink,
The fevered frenzy passed.

He was half alive,
Grinning in his misery.

THAT FEELING OF CHRISTMAS

An appetite left unsatisfied

Grows all-consuming;

Like a forest fire it rages,

Scarring the mind's landscape

With wanton visions.

Fingers too long in solitude,

A tongue, bitten and twisted,

Languishing to feast on burning coals

And the taste of hollow lust.

No relief in fevered dreams,

Awakening swollen with desire,

Breathless, shaken,

Restless visions, eyes unfocused.

A sound echoes in the dark,

Soul-stirring emptiness,

A forgotten voice, unmistakably familiar

From another life, perhaps.

A solitary, hastening heartbeat,

Wild in a freedom

That feels like Christmas.

HEARTPRINT

I've done all I could
To wash the traces of
Your fingertips from my skin.
So, tell me,
How do I erase the ways
Your heartprint
Stained the inside of my chest?

Wasted time, and memories
I can't recall.
Come to think of it,
I can't remember you at all
Stealing the sun from my sky,
Leaving
Only shadows in my mind.

Now the moon glows
Behind a veil of clouds,
Warmer dreams and glimpses of moments
Hidden from view.

Your fragrance
Lingers in the air,
Speechless—
A touch I've never known.

Eyes closed,
Drifting from consciousness,
Weightless—
Perhaps tomorrow I'll find relief.

JAGGED CHARM

See how the landscape's jagged charm

Draws you in

The way love has cut

And scarred this desert heart?

Too many times I have embraced acid tears

And pulled razor-edged words deep

Below this barren surface.

I have come to relish the pain,

Find comfort in the suffering.

Do your worst;

Bring me to my knees.

I will stand bloody and bruised

With the same smile

I brought to this torturous journey.

You have taught me well

How to survive

On less than what a bird needs.

See the bones beneath my skin;

Watch the veins pulse in time.

The ebb and flow of seasons,

Numb and delirious,

Are unwavering in the dark.

APOLOGIES

I'm sorry I was late;
I tried to find you sooner.
I've searched for you
Longer than I can remember.

I wanted so badly
To save you from the wreckage,
Keep you from losing
One more piece of yourself,
One more heartache,
One more disaster
Leaving you shaken to your core.

I'd like to believe
I could have made a difference
In another time, another chapter,
Of this tragedy.

Sadly, I arrived in the aftermath
When your faith in humanity,
Your hope of something real,
Had been reduced to ash.

You'd already poured out
Your last chance
On the lips of a man
Who never saw your worth;
You bled yourself dry
Over his jaded heart.

Now, you sit isolated,

A shell of what you were meant to be

Sustained on the bitterness he fed you.

Sometimes we find the one,

But we are a lifetime too late.

MY RESURRECTION

She had a way of being my resurrection.

Ripped from the grip of darkest nights,

Rescued with love on her breath,

Freely given another day in her sun.

Released from the fear of doubt,

She soothed my fevered brow

With the sweetest kiss;

Then in the breaking dawn,

I awoke alone.

Tangled in a memory and frozen sheets,

I shook myself to life and carried on.

The daily ritual began yet again.

DARK EYES

In the heat of a sultry summer night,

Racing heartbeats,

Shiny skin

In the wanton moonlight

Wrap me in pages of the story

Of your heart.

Drain my soul into your loving cup,

Take my everything,

Make you whole.

Pieces of me scatter;

You are a super nova

Sending a riptide through my universe.

I may come undone,

I won't deny anything you might ask,

I await your summer rain to pour on me.

Bring your flood over me in the morning darkness,

Bring comfort to me on sleepless nights,

I am a child in your warm glow.

One more breath and my senses unravel

With your touch,

One more brush and my heart stirs,

My head spins.

I am addicted to you;

You are my drug of choice.

A lifetime from all the reeling,

Shrouded in angelic feelings,

Happiness that feels so tidal,

Enraptured in a kiss so primal.

WIDE OPEN

I want to blow all this wide open
To the top of the world.
I was hoping
A blah a day would help
Ease the heartache,
Mend the scars.

Sometimes it's too much to take;
I'm used to salt in a wound,
A slap in the face,
When a taste of kindness
Is all I crave.

A smile on my face
And music in my ear,
Questioning intent,
Cautious out of fear.

Excuse the last few lines,
I've merely been living my life
Blind.

The day burns away until the fire dims,
Stars wink as the moon demands attention;
She will pull at the tides of your life,
Raise you beyond your breaking point.

She slips silently below the horizon
In an ancient dance. Fire into embers,
The heat of her glow
Will have you restless,

Tangled in empty sheets,
Reduced to ash.

Craving a drop
From her luminous skin
The ocean knows her ways;
Listen to it roar,
Beating fists upon the rocks,
Never getting enough,
Insatiable.

SILENT WHISPER

I wake up confused,
Naked on the floor,
Ashamed of what was said
And done the night before.

I listen to the rain,
Chaos on the roof,
Whispered voices
Lament this broken fool.

I keep my eyes shut tight,
I drown in guilty pleasures,
Wishing to start all over;
These pieces were always mine,
Never yours.

A cancer in my chest,
A desert for a heart,
Barren behind these eyes,
Wasted from the start.

Nothing left to salvage,
Nothing here to save,
Just a room of broken memories
Alone in this grave.

One last *I love you*
A cobweb on your lips.
Our house, burned to the ground,
Silent and cold as winter's grip.

DYING DAILY

Find what you love and let it kill you;
What I love has killed me daily.

Somehow I wake
From the same twisted dream.

Rescued in my final heartbeat,
I am resurrected

Only to feel the blades of a thousand knives,
Shred my soul.

As I lay on this altar willingly,
I come back to the same moment.

I refuse the blindfold;
Let me see your eyes

As you lay waste to me again.
I have no fear left;

I have come to see
This is how love works.

It strips me to dust and bones,
Then I awaken on my funeral pyre.

SHE IS A STORM

Lightning in her gaze,

Thunder in her voice,

She leaves devastation.

Completely undone,

You find yourself dangling

Half-alive from the fallout.

You pray for rain,

She will bring you drought or flood.

In each and every aftermath

You find yourself rebuilding,

Hoping she will destroy you again.

In the fading light,

We feel

The teeth of our mortality

Sink in.

We anticipated

Our skin would break

With each passing decade,

Yet each time

We escaped more confident.

Now in the twilight, our bones

Can feel the rip and tear.

MORNING COFFEE

I stand in the doorway

Watching you sip your coffee,

The way your little hands cradle the cup,

How your thumbs gently stroke the rim;

I love the way the morning light,

Shines brightly in your dark eyes.

Out the back porch you watch

Waves crash a stone's throw away,

You are lost

Miles and miles from here;

Thoughts and memories

Swirl inside that pretty head of yours.

I want to ask you where you've been,

But deep inside

I know I do not need to know;

You are in a place no one can touch,

Free from pain, free from the chains.

I'd love to be

The warm, dark fluid you put to your lips;

You sip it down so slow and pleasing.

I understand how much you want

To heat the places that have been cooling

For years and years.

My words only go so far,

My touch nowhere near enough,

My love deeper than you've known before,

But is it what you really need?

You have never been cold,

But there's a distance in your love.

Could it be fear?

Are you gun shy from years of heartache?

The middle of winter,

January is a fitting time

To pull your sweater tight

And absorb the morning light.

I know you love me,

I have no doubts;

In the same breath, I realize

I may never completely have you.

There are pieces of you

Left in crooked frames

Boxed on dusty closet shelves.

You have never known a gentle hand

Only needing what the moment asked;

I hunger to show you

Places with memories

Captured inside a golden hue,

Like the moment the sun kisses the horizon.

Warmth in small moments

Shapes perceptions into better times.

APRIL 10

Mississippi fields blanketed
With a buzzing honey swarm
Come alive in the blooming spring.
Mile after mile, the road noise
Escalates into a manic hive
Of words and pictures I husband,
Collecting nectar
From the banks of rust-colored rivers
Reflecting a Monet landscape
Slightly out of focus.

They moan their stories
With a velvet drawl;
No hurry beneath the sleepy-eyed sun,
Still two months out from showing
How little mercy is held in its gaze.
Blacktop fringed with Indian Paintbrushes,
Bloodstained marches await kerosene nights
That glow miles from here
Down paths only the innocent find
And the crooked create;
A seductive element
Always in the periphery,
Like the bead of sweat
On a salty bronze neck and collarbone
Exposed for temptation's sake.

This land is soft,

Finger deep with promise and possibility,

But the mouth of a thirsty river is insatiable;

She wants your soul,

Hearts are decorative garnish

With little purpose but ceremony.

Read the curving hills and shades of green

Like promises never kept.

Her voice is silent to masses,

Yet candy to the ones awake;

Listen to her reverie

And you'll lose your fear of time.

She is timeless.

She has the patience to wear you down,

Make you crawl,

Then bury you in your father's sins.

A raindrop on August asphalt

Evaporates in the darkness;

Too much time to think

Amidst the hum of Highway 78.

Melodious whispers run

From a life endured

And one attempting to survive

The last hard frost.

THORNY ROSE

She sees right through

The facade you have come to accept

As *your* truth—

All languid pills and nagging reality

You are still a lifetime from swallowing.

Break your own heart

On your own time.

She has better dreams

Brewing on kitchen counters

A thousand miles from what you've known

Or seen.

And just so you know, it's beautiful,

This pocket-sized preserver

She carries in her chest;

You don't deserve the fading light

She leaves on your windowsill,

But you'll reach for it anyway.

It's in your nature to reach

For the thorny rose,

But you'll never hold it;

You'll never love her

Like she loves you,

So write a eulogy to the sunrise.

As the smoke rises

From her river,

You are washed away from

Everything you thought

You wanted.

PERCEPTION

Are we more than our perception?

More than the landscape

We greet through frosted windowpanes,

Always speaking our skewed view

Of what a wandering heart

Could be, should be, would be

If we had the resolve

To walk the path less traveled?

I am wretched with guilt

Even if it isn't mine.

The picture from my childhood

Framed on a canary yellow wall

Reassured me all could be saved

If I only had enough faith,

A belief in something grand,

Something pure.

The older I get,

The less I find grand,

The less I see pure.

Tainted in daylight,

Shrouded in what sin tastes like,

The sweetest nectar

And every bit a carcinogen

Swallows me breath by weighted breath.

The sum of what we witness in tragedy
And triumph accumulates,
Fingerprints stain our dreams,
Press our armor into rice paper wings.

We rise, soaring until flame and fury
Leave us grounded once again
With hands that were never ours,
Borrowed from an ancestor

Whose name was erased
From every tongue before us.
And now we write words
Shadowed with history

We never lived,
Never read, never heard—
But we write it all the same.
Leaving volumes on shelves

That will return to the dust
We were created from.
This story,
Unwritten and unrecognizable

To the child you once were,
You once raised.
Still, the story resounds,
Mundane and glorious.

Without the bitter,

Would we know the sweet?

What is cherished

Was once thought lost

To the fire of life,

Washed into the storm,

Ripped from fearful fingers,

Before weeping eyes and trembling lips.

It is safe to say goodbye

And anticipate the new hello.

CLUTCHING WORDS

I am clutching your words,
You are everything I've ever hoped for.

Phrases and fragments
Have slipped away like dandelion wishes;
Is it any wonder I am blind to my own self-worth?

I have carelessly given slivers of myself
As your words splintered,
Embedding in this hollow heart.

Now swollen with an infection,
My heart is suspended,
Caught forever in a fragile moment.

LEAP YEAR

A freefall leap of faith
Netless highwire walk,
With no thought of turning back
As the flames consume
Everything once solid.
Substance and gravity
Tethered only to what is felt in the soul,
Only what is felt with the soul.

Starlight and new moons
Birth tomorrow's paths while I sit
Thirty thousand feet above city lights
Spread out like constellations
Cutting through clouds like a winter storm.
Outside the muffled window
Play memories of 1976.

In the back of an Oldsmobile station wagon,
Hypnotized by the humming wheels
And fresh graveled asphalt
Pointing east through the heart of America,
A young head fills with dreams he never knew
Could someday cover our skin with tattoos
Only meant for your eyes.

Leap turns to leapt,
The rush of reality
No one believed tangible
Now fills the belly,
Brightens the eyes,

And sings

The morning sun to life.

The line between inspiration and madness

Tangles between fingers,

Collects phrases,

And paints a highway

Stretched out for the next quarter century.

A silent symphony behind a naked chest,

Breathless and beating.

CUMBERLAND GAP

Low clouds cling, painted in hallways
Of oak and evergreen.
We are set aflame with liquid fire
Could've beens in ruby throats and diamond eyes.
Can you survive
The desolation of angels and their jagged shine?

Meant for remembering
In a world built for lost memories,
I am merely a lightning strike
Swallowed in darkness,
A ripple breaking on stones
Before it touches the shore.

Born in a time before time meant a damn thing,
Before a man tried to tame
What was never meant to be tamed,
The fool who tried
To rule a wildness
Better left to its own devices.

Can you feel the pull,
The part of you
Never meant to submit to a chain?
Even a cobweb is too restrained
For blowing eyelashes and finding feathers
Touchstones along our path.

EDEN

Before the fall
We were bathed in pure light,
Eyes brighter than the sun,
Mouths created for pleasure.
But once our eyes tasted the darkness,
Our hearts began to lust.

Thrown from the garden
Ready to fulfill every desire,
Build an empire
For what we believed to be love.
Searching for a way home,
We were torn
Between the angels and devils of Eden.

RATTLE OF CHAINS

The rattle of chains,
The click of a lock
Echo in this empty room,
Shadows of evening
Constant.
Held helpless,
I have learned
Not to struggle.

I feel each link
Dig into my flesh;
I gaze into the darkness,
Eyes hungry,
I await your approach.
Dangling words
Never murmured
Leave me wanton,
Speechless and dizzy.

You stand before me,
Key in your cruel hand;
Pressing it to your lips,
You swallow
My last drop of hope
With the coldest of smiles,
Then turn
And fade into my memory.

THE GAZE

He cannot count the times

He would walk into a room

And find her gazing silently out a window.

So many punishing thoughts

Rushed through his mind,

His heart tore

Imagining where she longed to be.

Was it freedom?

Was it her past?

Was it a million miles from here,

From him,

From his passionless hands?

Each time he pictured her staring

He died a little more,

Until one day he knew

He would only find a tearstained note

Where she last lingered

Alone in this cage,

Flightless

And afraid to fall.

SPLINTERS

I am but splinters
Of what I could have been;
There is no need for you
To try and understand who I am.

You will go mad
Searching the labyrinth
In which I have hidden my heart.

Do you see the garden in winter?
I am the ghosts of flowers;
If you push too deep,
You will be left with empty hands.

It is no fault of your own;
Empathy will not help you
Beneath these murky depths.

Maybe I should be sorry.
What came before you has gilded this heart,
It is pointless to scale these walls
Just to wander this desert.

I am trying to save you
From endless sorrow;
Take what little you have gathered and run

Back to the possibilities of a life
With greens and gold.
The only thing here is washed-out gray
And heartbreak.

ROOM SERVICE

She daydreamed of room service,

Drunken nights in hotel rooms,

Travel at the drop of a hat.

Let the wind carry her where it would,

Living novels

Instead of reading someone else's version.

She could get lost in a stranger's eyes,

See every page they tried to cut,

Her appetite larger than the mundane,

Captivating, seductive.

Sex wasn't the payoff,

Secrets were;

She longed to be their priestess.

Show me how deep you go;

Years of splashing puddles,

Created a thirst for the darkest of oceans, she said.

Most never made it past waist-high water;

She grew bored, then slipped away

As he checked himself in the mirror behind the bar.

A shooting star,

She shone like the sun.

WHERE I STAND

I may not be where I'd hoped to be,

But I am here,

In pursuit of my goals and dreams.

Currents shift, relentless;

We make choices to fight or flow.

After many years of fighting,

I am slowly learning to flow.

Not to say I have no direction

Or I can't adjust my sails to get

Where I believe I need to be.

When you are open to possibilities

You never imagined,

Life can truly surprise you.

I may not be where I'd hoped to be,

But I am a grateful man

Blessed with a certainly uncertain future

Who will always see sunshine after a storm.

II. DEFINING

PAINTED VISIONS

My God, how you paint
These visions in my mind;
Glimpses of this faded soul,
Days washed into oblivion.

Your voice sedates me,
Whispering, *It has always been you.*

Though I remember it never really was me,
I willingly play the part of distraction
From the madness you embraced
Instead of these arms,
Leaving you sweaty, speechless, breathless.

Yes, I loved you.
Yes, I love you.

I am enfolded in this tragedy
With no way to escape.
In my defense,
I could have made a difference
Given any real chance.

No matter how you convinced yourself,
I was not like all the others;
I was actually
A giver.

RESTART

It is never easy to start anew,

Find a place to pack away,

Old dusty memories,

And make room for hope.

They use the word "fresh" for new beginnings.

However, there comes a time

When boxes line the hallway,

You are buried in bones and scrap paper,

And the concept "fresh" no longer fits.

"Fresh" is the last word that comes to mind.

There have been many chapters

In this old heart;

I am a hoarder

Who holds onto frayed pieces of string.

There are days

I want to set fire to this house

And walk away

From everything I have known.

I peer out dingy windows,

Imagine how bright the world could be;

Then I blink

And nothing has really changed at all.

TWILIT INTERSECTION

In the twilight we intersect.

Vaporous,
Cutting the sky,
Showing our scars,
Unknowingly
Looking for common ground.

A moment passes,
Sinking into the horizon
We are unchanged,
Though never the same.

Tilting axis,
Trajectory forever altered,
Destined for so much more
Than spoon-fed mediocrity.

Clouds, like waves in an ocean,
Slowly roll toward the horizon;
Lose yourself in the silent current,
Mind set adrift...timeless.

Speak the confessions of your soul
Carried through the grand expanse;
The healing begins
And I am spent.

Grateful for these moments,

Good and bad, trials and the triumphs;

Without the hardest of times

Golden moments would never be so sweet.

We all share shades of heartache.

SHADES OF HEARTACHE

Whether splinters of moments
Or the laceration of years,
The deeper the love,
The more tender the scars.

Belief in healing
Crumbles
Under the weight of a song,
A familiar fragrance.

Each of us walk along
A well-traveled path of senses
Trying to forget fragments of yesterdays
Until the dust settles upon what we bury.

Behind a smile
Lies every tearstained goodbye
That started with the taste of possibility
And the sound of forever.

THE SPARK

The smallest spark begins smoldering

With a breath of conversation,

A flame in the dark

On the periphery.

The warmth grows into heat

As the language sweetens;

Seductive songs open deafened ears

And an intoxicating smile.

This fire glows,

Slowly burning from the inside out,

So consumed you can taste the intensity,

The unending desire.

Sacrificing heart and soul,

Brought to your knees,

Enraptured in the pleasure

And pain a touch brings,

You are incinerated inside their words

Until you rise like a phoenix

From the ashes of passion.

THE PREACHER

Damnation

Salvation

The preacher preaches

To the only soul he'll never save;

Behind the window he watches

The world shake and fall.

Crucified

Justified

The singer sings

For the heart caged in his chest,

Every note warbled

Behind the beat.

Bruising

Blushing

A writer writes

For the call of the flame,

The burning of dark-eyed, lucid muses

Swallowed in the witching hour.

Consuming

Enraptured

A painter paints

From a godlike shroud of passion,

Enveloped in a fevered dream,

Alive in every stroke.

Kindled
Beautiful

CREASES IN THE CLOUDS

Maybe we are meant to be
The creases in the clouds,
Rays cutting through the swaddled grey,
The space between the raindrops,
Reflections of warmth
Like a feather bed
On a biting winter night.

Mercy unwavering,
Arms extended for the wailing child,
Tearstained moments of grace,
Digging deeper than where we've been,
Some scars are reminders
Of alleys better left behind.

There's a blue
That breathes hope into our wings,
Stops the free fall just before impact,
Brings blossoms from a deep frost
To gentle furrowed rows,
Soaking seeds of dreams
In optimistic revelry.

Here we go,
Changing,
Evolving,
A blooming resurrection
Embraces what we cannot see,
The beauty in a broken space.

ENDLESS BLUE

And then

There are days

Without even a whisper of a cloud.

No need for a silver lining,

The blue sky is as endless

As a child's imagination

Soaking up the warmth of the sun—

A quiet reprieve

From the shadows of winter,

One step closer to spring

When the new season of life will begin.

Smile,

Enjoy the transition,

Know in your heart

Better days are on the horizon.

CIGARETTE GLOW

I wake to the glow of your cigarette

And watch as you

Blow smoke rings

Around the moon.

Constellations pale

As you sit beneath them

And I can't take my eyes off you.

Music plays inside my head

A symphony of inspiration you create;

Oh, how you make my heart race.

Words fail me;

Gibberish

The only words I can find.

You drift towards me;

I reach for you,

You slide your slender hand into mine.

In your arms,

Safe as a song inside a dream,

Moments are lost

In the darkness.

You hold me

Closer than a breath,

Like a narcotic through my veins.

We fall together

Under the sheets,

A tangle of colors

In a tapestry of shadow.

SHAKEN MORTALITY

We were never more alive
Than the times our mortality was shaken
At the prospect of losing everything
We cherished in a withering exhale.
We began to feel a little deeper,
Remembered minute moments
Crisp with clarity and jagged with detail.
We loved harder, wept with passion,
Held our loved ones a little longer.

We fade back to the default
Position of mediocracy much too easily;
As days burn away in the aftermath,
Tragedy yellows in the sunlight.

We pretended it was enough,
But was it?
Is it?
When a wound scars over
Does it become less important?
Do we deny our daily remorse?
If we, in fact, clutch pain endlessly,
Does it constitute lack of growth?

I suppose my question is,
Can there be a wrong way
To live through a severing loss?

I am not you and you are not me;
I do not pretend to know

How anyone else processes grief.

Some bury and others bleed for years,

Some refuse to move on

From the lightning strike,

Choosing to feed the insatiable mouth of death.

I believe the best way to show your love

Is to carry on and use the devastation

As a catalyst to live an inspired life,

To make a difference with the time we have left.

No one truly knows

How many grains of sand

Sift through our hourglass.

RAVENOUS

She is a raven...ravenous.

A touch of madness

Turned paper hearts into confetti,

Chipped away at my frozen soul,

Swept this mess away into the night

Along with all these wasted words.

More than bent, less than broken,

I am suspended between

The sunrise and a faded dream;

I am the scar of a tattoo

Long ago removed,

Discolored, disfigured,

The great disconnect.

ILLUSIONS

I have seen the illusion of walking on water before,

And every time I was left to drown.

If you are another beautiful liar,

Tell me you are different, and I shall believe.

You will not hear a sound from me;

The air is so much sweeter,

Kisses so much wetter,

Moments I could not feel this heart.

Opened like a can of heartbreak,

I never knew oblivion

Was the perfect place to start.

I was broken when you found me, set adrift.

You have turned every scar into a beautiful tattoo

Colorful, like sunbeams

Shining through waterfall mist.

Every day you find a new way to paint it all.

I love your color,

The way you look against this white canvas;

I'll share this portrait of eternity

Lost in your arms.

All I knew before was doing time,

Your selfless charm brought me life,

I have surrendered to this fate.

No one ever tried to save me before.

You swam to the deepest waters,

I am rescued by your love.

SUBJECTIVE

They say to write what you know,

But the more I live, the less I know.

My day job

Requires just enough attention

To let thoughts and ideas

Simmer all day on the back burner.

I let them marinate

Until I make sense of the alphabet soup,

Then I pour them on this keyboard,

A symphony of utter chaos.

There are days I wonder

If I have gone completely mad;

Only a madman would make

Paper airplanes from his words

And sail them into a world

That never asked to read them.

I force my visions into their mouths, their ears;

Sometimes I see what was needed,

Other times I witness the scribe

Disappear into the abyss.

I try to read and understand other writers' pieces,

Let their words tickle my ears,

Open my eyes to differing perspectives.

I admire the focus

Of my fellow writers;

How they map things out

Then strive towards that end.

Yet, here I am back to this soup,
Pushing myself into the ground
Praying for a glorious ending.

THE AFTERGLOW

It begins with a whisper,

A kiss, a giggle, that look,

Then fever flushes the skin.

Try as one might, eyes cannot lie;

They slowly close

Beneath hair that muffles words

Between heart and soul,

Moments meant for the one

Revealed in splendid detail

Unseen by the naked eye.

A tidal wave crashes

In the deepest places

Never before woken

With less than a divine caress.

Once again, I am speechless

Inside the afterglow.

COUNTING GRAINS OF SAND

It has been 696 days since your final goodbye
Left me in a disarray.

There were many sleepless nights
I believed it was inside my head.

41,760 minutes alone
Inside this fractured skull.

I've found intimacy with strangers,
Keeping my numbed mind distracted.

This bloody mess unrecognizable,
All the pieces need to be repaired.

You silently stole them
Then slipped into your new lover's mouth.

Suspended without gravity,
I lost my tether.

Waiting for the ground to rush up and greet me,
The glorious imploding debris.

You scraped me from the bottom of your shoe,
I was easily discarded in the apathy.

250,560 seconds and counting,
My demise infinitely finite.

I am wasted breath.

THAT MOMENT

Who knows that moment,

That split second

When love hits like lightning

In the darkest of times?

Who has more than they need

Of what makes life

Worth the tears and the pain?

The struggle for a heart deep enough

To drink from for eternity

Is my heart's cry.

You have answered every tear

With patience and tenderness;

A kiss which

No mortal man has ever known

And angels have only dreamt.

That moment you bring,

Like stars in the winter sky,

Countless.

HEART OF SATURDAY NIGHT

Is this the heart of Saturday night?

High on serenity,

Spent melodies, and dopamine,

She glimmers behind a dime store veil,

A treasure to seduce and swallow the ruin.

There is always a siren just out of view,

Yet we stare a minute too long,

Hypnotized by the darkness;

She is alive and holds promises never to be kept,

The chance to be who you wished you were.

A landscape built for strangers,

Occupy the pavement in your Sunday best,

Intoxicated smiles, and bridges yet to burn;

Alive in the moment,

But reckless and restless.

Wet with desperation, losing oneself

Beneath the neon, pelvis-pulsing low end,

You are brilliant in your second skin,

Your guard down,

Humanity laid bare.

Long chains with jagged crosses,

A hint of country

But speaking city scripture;

Run from your roots,

Rootless.

Shaken by the storm in shades of blue,

The shadows of steel and concrete scrape the skies.

Summer sweats and winter weeps,

Cold honey drips

From dark eyes and parting lips.

Mr. Waits no longer lingers

In the light of the four-way;

He danced into the impending dawn

Creasing the skyline

With careful intent.

QUESTIONS OF LOVE

Do you really love me,
Or is it the thought of love?

Captivated by fantasy,
Snared by pretty pictures inside your head,
Seduced by the words of a love poem.
My love is not pretty;
It can be filthy at times.

Can you stay suspended in mutilation,
The lacerated carnage of a poisoned past?

If you cannot find the beauty in my torment,
How can you feel entitled to my golden sunsets?

Taste my bitter and my sweet,
Dig deep for my glow,
Find the comfort of my dark spaces.

Can you accept ghosts
Who refuse eviction?

Would you purge my soul
And become my rapture?

I am not easy.

Below these stones which have been thrown,
Piled high around this hole in my chest,
There can be a new life,
A new love.

It will take more than patience and selflessness;
I have more stubborn than most can handle.

This road is not for the weary,
Though many have tried
And been left twisted,
Unrecognizable.

PROPAGATE

To propagate the July ghost

In the jaws of January

Crippling beneath the wolf moon,

Howling.

Ravens freckle the landscape,

Watching the shaking hand

Reach for anything bent

To release this burning memory.

In the tongue aflame,

In a bridled voice,

Lie redemption of a heartbreak;

There is no way to stop the coming undone.

Set your flesh upon the altar,

Speak a blessing,

Whisper a cursed *Hallelujah*,

Feel your spine respond.

Heavy breath and wicked ways

Roll from lips of wanton fever,

Bitten, bleeding,

Bruised like Heaven's kiss.

Does the name illuminate the darkness?

Does the brush stroke

Paint the remembering

Shaded with blushed cheeks and a sweaty throat?

Unleashed and unrepentant, some rivers run hot

Beneath a season of ice and snow,

Surrendered to the way

The sun always rises.

FALLING LINGUISTICS

Words are always falling,

Like autumn's fire,

Somber and sweet like predawn rain.

We catch the flavor of each syllable

On our tongues,

Swallow what we will never fully comprehend

In a constant state of flux.

The rhythm navigates our days

Into restless nights,

Swollen dreams of flames

Refuse to be extinguished.

Waking with questions on our lips,

Bruises on our throat,

The voice we once believed to be ours

Is now forsaken,

So we scratch out our storyline—

A coded epitaph for ears that never listen,

Eyes that never open.

Show me your palm,

I will celebrate your history,

The journey you have endured.

Not everyone gets to bathe

In the glow of a red-letter day;

Most don't understand

The magic lingers in the periphery,

Rarely straight ahead.

Blink, and it will evaporate,

Morning dew in the warming sun.

A soul feeds

On moments of gratitude and wonder;

We wither in the blindness we are fed,

Growing older and more sightless.

Our dimming vision

Is the most tragic of all slow deaths,

But even in the harshest of places

Possibility can blossom.

THE SAVIOR

So, you believed you saved me,

Rescued me from my despair;

You must have one hell of a Messiah complex.

How do you save someone

While never holding their hand,

Never embracing a pain,

Never kissing a tear?

By keeping them bound to a ghost,

Hostage to a hope

That will never be realized?

You constantly run from your chances,

Push away every cloud on the horizon.

If you never truly wanted me,

Why the elaborate ruse?

Was it the need for a fall guy?

Someone to be there when you ran out of options?

I am only human,

And a poor example at times.

I bleed,

I feel,

I need,

I have desires that will never come to be.

My heart is overgrown

With barbs and thistle;

You were my last chance at something more.

Now there is nothing,

The deconstruction has begun,

A set up from the start.

Mangled in the aftermath,

I am unrecognizable to anyone

Who came before you.

My hollowed shell is all that remains.

BREATH OF BUKOWSKI

The way it happened
Was something even Bukowski
Wouldn't have lived through.
The torment of a soul, exquisite
Flames burned brilliantly,
Consumed,
Embraced the killing.

Alcohol-induced numbness reduces the resistance,
Yet the disfigured reflection remains.
Like watching your nose bleed
Spattering into a porcelain sink,
Mesmerized by the changing canvas
Streaking,
Crawling toward the drain.

Frozen and captivated,
Life in slow-motion,
Admiration for my creation,
A massacre from this dizzying height.
I smile with pride;
I have withstood onslaught
From the devil's worst nightmare.

They must have missed the memo;
This darkness is where I was born.
I only feel ugly in the light, you fool.
Cheers to you, pitchfork whore—
I am still breathing.

Only slightly

...but breathing just the same.

DEVASTATION

Some people want

A love that devastates,

Something that will

Rearrange their landscape,

Cause tsunamis,

And leave them twisted in the wreckage

Only to lament

When the earthquake subsides

And the ground

Beneath their feet

Ceases rolling.

They are left alone

In maddening silences,

Left to wrestle

The Whys of the aftermath;

They would much rather

Remain ravaged

By the natural disaster

Than sit quietly

In their own company.

BALANCE

We search for balance

Between want and need.

The desire to be wanted,

To find someone who ignites our passion.

Want can fuel our very bones,

Coming to the ledge high above Need,

Poised on the adrenaline-filled precipice

Trying not to be someone else's air,

Only their fire—a piece of their story.

To be their subtle 2 a.m. smile

On a dark highway, driving aimlessly,

Trying to remember the reason

They endured yet another gray dream.

Yes, I say it is better to be wanted than needed.

Wanted is known to be temporary,

Only sustained for a short time,

Ending with the least amount of damage;

Needed leads to true devastation,

And the scars of a nuclear winter.

IMMORTAL YOUTH

Oh, the taste of immortal youth.
To be the resilient gladiator
Running headlong into the fray of battle,
The grandeur of becoming a war hero,
The fresh honeyed kiss of love.

Lying in scarless arms
Those tempting eyes, dark and inviting,
Lips unstained with disillusion
Passing lovers who flash like shooting stars,
Countless and brilliant in their uniqueness
With no time for death or dying.

Forever is a possibility,
So, dream your dreams,
Move your mountains,
Wrestle your angels,
Slay the demons of your darkest nights.

Yesterday is still fresh as morning dew,
Tomorrow, merely a second thought,
But today is yours to bend and shape,
So, shine on.

LOSS OF WORDS

I have run out of words for you.

Speechless,

I hold no whisper of a thought,

I have pleaded with you for the final time,

I am no one's lazy Sunday,

I am no one's breakfast in bed,

Midnight stroll,

Midday coffee shop conversation.

I am a temporary melancholy smile

That sneaks upon your lips

A month after summer has passed.

I am that old sweatshirt he left behind

You want to ritualistically burn,

Yet cannot bear the thought of losing

For the fear of forgetting

The faint fragrance of his essence.

Losing that last memento

Would mean losing every trace

That what you had was more

Than merely a college girl's daydream.

Stop trying to embrace

This grey coastal rain,

Go out and discover

That bolt of blue

You were meant to be

Wrapped around.

III. MINUTE

THE DREAM

I had a dream last night that I died;
I fell from the skies into a field of tall grass.

Everything moved in slow-motion,
Nothing was completely clear,
Faces felt familiar yet had no definition.
I am uncertain how I knew I was dead
Except for the sorrow I tasted
Was unlike anything I've known;
A feeling of being lost with no chance of being found.

I called your name
As I wept,
The only sound a heart-wrenching moan.
In this moment I realized
You were truly gone forever,
I would never know another moment of joy,
Time became insignificant, stagnant.

I looked at my hands;
They were horribly stained.
In disbelief, I attempted to wash them clean
With no success.
This sense of helplessness
Was a weight too heavy to bear;
My heart began to separate from the grief.

I woke in tears,
Sobbing for your soothing touch.

MUSIC HEALS

Music is a healer,

Whether Coltrane

Settles over a smooth scotch,

The Delta blues

Feeds your soul,

Or Tom Waits

Plays languidly as you type your darkest secrets,

The pieces of you

Never meant for the light of day.

Like a movie,

Our lives have a soundtrack;

Though we don't realize it in the moment,

Songs play in the background,

Hide in memories,

Stand in a crowded room

Beneath the dull roar.

A song you have never known before,

Opens each scar of your fractured heart,

Tying knots

Where those damn butterflies should be

And in the depths

Releases an avalanche of yesterdays.

Then Jack Johnson sets you on a beach

With nothing but blue skies;

The thought of tomorrow

Has a little less melancholy.

Music can rescue

Even the most hopeless of us all.

Lay back at the end of a brutal day

With a deep breath,

Let the gods of music kiss you,

Exhale the melody,

Awaken with a fresh vision.

The rhythm of life will always sway,

Finding the beat in each coming day.

THE ART OF KISSING

Some kisses are left bitter on the tongue,

Others are forgotten in some darkened dream,

Never shared in the aftermath of goodbye.

I know you have tasted them,

Both salty and sweet, toe-curling and sour;

Memories of what I had left to offer,

Regret for our jagged end.

I admit I'm wrapped in trepidation

Over how I have drifted,

How deep I've buried my heart these last few years.

I pray you feel the difference,

How this was never meant to be the same.

This starting over

A new beginning

This one has no final page;

It has an unending language,

A storyline that will linger long after we are gone.

This eternal kiss will erase anything that came before;

An art form that strips the canvas of every stain,

A dance that resets the heart's rhythm,

A slow dance for the soul.

Breathe me in,

Cradle my name in your lungs forever.

SHADOWS OF A KISS

There are kisses
Meant to be remembered
As sweet as
The first time
You held a lover's hand.

Fingers locked,
Tongues tangled,
Pins and needles,
Eyes closed.

In slow-motion,
The taste
Of a new fire

So wild
It burns
The deepest creases
Of your soul,

So fresh
You replay
Every moment
On a thousand
Solitary
Winter nights.

A LONG DRIVE

The things I think about on long drives.

I wish you could have felt how much you were loved, how you affect-
ed each soul moved by your beauty. I suppose we all have some Helen
Keller in our makeup. Deaf, blind, and mute to how much we mean to
others, we get so buried in our own self defeat that we never see the sun-
rise, or the way the storm brought out the blooms of life. In our eyes it's
just more rain, more muck and mire.

We have lost too many to the void, and the despair settles in our veins.
Can we take the time to remember how we were shaken to our core by
the loss of someone we never thought would be gone in an instant? Do
we want to transfer devastation to the ones we share our world with?
Because that is, in fact, what each of us do. Even unknowingly, our im-
pact, as well as our leaving, can cause a hollow too long to heal from,
so the cycle of grief and despair continues. More sparrows fall to the
ground, lifeless and hopeless.

We need to bind together in our humanity and see how connected we
are to one another. I feel loss the same as you. In our undoing, it is okay
to lie down broken. We all need to recenter and find our feet again. In
the same breath, we need to recognize those who have been lying next
to us in pain and show some compassion, some kindness—help them to
their feet when they are ready. And until that time, we need to lie with
them in the darkness, our heartbeats the beacon, the home fire, burn-
ing in the distance to keep the taste of hope on their tongue.

Isolation will only sever our own hearts, cripple our own hands, and
bind our own feet to anchors, pulling us further from the light.

Be the spark in the storm,

The life you help could be your own.

DIVE BAR

Leaving the corner dive bar,

The crisp night air

Cools the heat generated by

Drinks and conversations.

Flickering neon,

Staggering laughter,

High heels clicking on concrete,

Wrestling on a loosely tied long coat.

Arm locked with a new connection

Debating whether to weave the city streets

Or catch the subway home.

Tonight is not a night to be alone;

Too many broken songs

Whistle through this skyscraper skyline.

Better to be holed up on the fifteenth floor,

Dim lights,

A new bottle of rye,

Smeared lipstick,

Memories burning into our consciousness.

The fresh spark of a new beginning

Can be addictive;

Memorize the moments,

The tastes, the smells.

They will serve you well

When your overpriced flat

Becomes as cold and empty

As the city streets below.

DRUNKEN MOUTHS

You come to me drunken,

Wet from the mouth of another,

Lie to me and tell me I'm like no other.

His words stir you,

I am a temporary fix;

You search the landscape

Looking for something to awaken your soul

Like I once did.

You may think me the fool,

You keep me hidden from your world,

A toy to play with at your leisure,

To use as you need me.

My heart is dispensable

Like common trash

You can bury

Or incinerate.

Still, I cling

To the moments we shared;

They bring me comfort

In my darkness.

Thinking we could have been more,

That I could have been

The one to bring you home,

Drunken and wet.

OLD LOVERS

Old lovers

Bring on melancholy smiles;

How happy she shines

Holding a new hand.

How he adores her,

Brushing feather-like hair from her face,

Tucking it behind her ear,

Giddy as she talks.

He is mesmerized

By the way her lips move,

Memorizing how each syllable

Slips from her tongue.

She paints memories

In pastel watercolors and morning light.

I remember those stories;

They are scenes

From my favorite movie.

A fly on the wall, I sit

Solitary in this old café

And witness

How she changes his life.

REUNION

How are you? he asked.

My god, it's been years.

You look great

but what the hell happened to you?

Where have you been?

You are more beautiful than I remember,

But there's a brokenness behind your eyes.

Well, she replied, *love has been a devastation.*

I have been rescued

From the crumbling edge of the abyss,

Taken to dizzying heights

Only to plummet with mangled wings

Shameless

On jagged rocks along an ocean shoreline,

A witness to my own crimson blood.

A slow thin flow

Down into a cocktail

Of scarlet salty tears.

Don't get me wrong,

I have no regrets;

I've lived a thousand lives,

These jewels lining my soul

Have stories,

The verses of legends

Immortal.

A PUNCH TO THE MOUTH

Everyone has a plan until they get punched in the mouth.
Mike Tyson

We step into the light with purpose, we see the goals within reach, we extend our faith-drenched hands. Then the blow comes from beyond the periphery. We are shaken; we question every choice we ever made. Where did we go wrong? What did we do to deserve this bloody mess? We must have made a mistake, right?

Maybe we just caught a glancing blow from something never intended for us; perhaps it was just a wakeup call to recenter and focus a little more. Negative moments aren't always about something we deserve or a setback to where we believe we belong. There are times shit just happens without being a payback.

These moments may be just a test of mettle, a way to see where our resolve is set, meant to steady our legs on a stormy sea so we can press forward into what our souls have been sailing toward. Something bigger than us, more than we could be selfishly—hearts hoping to impact the world around us, pushing for the positive ripple, the betterment of our surroundings.

Don't let a sucker punch destroy you. Rise from it, taste it fully, and carry on with more purpose than you ever have before. Life cannot always be calm waters, you will never withstand the storms if you never taste your own blood. We all bleed.

Make the struggle a catalyst, not a coffin;
You are more than the moment.

FOREST FOCUSED

I'm not entirely sure

When my focus

Went to the forest from the trees.

Could have been

A gradual pan of perspective,

The clearing of a blind spot

I didn't know existed

Until I woke up one day

With depth to my vision.

A two-dimensional world

Became a myriad

Of endless possibilities

Tangled in decisions

That are only mine to make,

Mine to live with, mine to revel in.

I have no fear of failure,

Only the fear of never taking the chance

To fall from all I've known.

Push through the pain of yesterday's bruises,

Let the taste of my own blood

Inspire tomorrow's sunrise.

We are never as alone

As when we awaken

From a monochrome dream,

Fresh eyes,

Crystalline sense of purpose
Warmed in the growing dawn.

Winter is the season of rebirth,
Summer still awaits the ones
Courageous enough
To embrace the flame,
Swallow the sun,
Anticipate the shadows,
Fade from the periphery.

RUSTY RIBBON OF TWILIGHT

As the last rusty ribbon of twilight
Is erased from the horizon

The milky way hangs
Like a choker around midnight's throat

Blooming stars
Twinkle and fade

Like yesterday's change
We swore we'd wear like tattoos

They wash out with the rain
That fell between dusk and dawn

Bitten tongue,
Bitten lip

Bloodied in fear or passion,
We tried to be brave

But this heart is gun shy
And runs at the sound of possibility

Braced up and broken,
Stronger than meets the eye

In the face of oblivion,
We stood

Awaiting fate's kiss of betrayal,
Here we are hesitant, yet hopeful

Spent,

Yet swallowed in faith

This moment of chrysalis is necessary

To ready ourselves for flight

Trust the metamorphosis,

Where this darkened state will bring you

It is not the end,

But the blossoming of brighter days

TEMPTATION

The problem with temptation

Is how easy it is to find

Around every corner,

Every curve in the road.

Whatever entices you

Will reappear

At the most inconvenient times,

Drive you to the edge of perdition,

Leave you naked

Stumbling, mumbling incoherently.

Hands scarred by weakness

Pray for redemption

You only taste temporarily;

Oh, how sweet trouble can be

When you are lost

In the fog it creates.

THE STORM

The storm,

The crashing wave,

The shoreline ever evolving,

The roar of a million pins

Dropped in a crescendo.

I feel shapeless and voiceless,

Numb in the coming night,

The pristine water

A torrential rain on a window,

Skewing a landscape

I memorized in a dream.

The errant perspective

My point of view

Is the only real truth to be found

When every witness tells a variation

Of the very same scene.

Our storylines reflect

The camera angles we are given.

What felt like falling

Turned out to be flight;

We are nothing if not consistent

In our miscalculations of depth

When reaching for a heart

Never meant to be held by familiar hands,

Yet fingerprints were left by ghosts

Lost in the changing tide,

Buried beneath,

Swallowed in blindness.

Faith was etched

On the inside of a bitten cheek

And love was found

Hung in a dreamcatcher

Around a bruised neck,

Birds sacrifice their feathers

For safe passage

Through hungry teeth

And lonely eyes.

I am not a martyr,

But more honest than you want to hear

In the face of breaking your own heart.

No need to sacrifice

Your vision of love

For a season of bitter winter,

Agape is the purest form of light.

WAGGING TONGUES

Let the tongues wag.

He drove until the road ran out,
And buried himself deep in the fault line.
His breathing slowed
As the sky was swallowed in the darkness,
Fearless,
Visionless,
Becoming clearer in his own undoing.

This path is tricky and treacherous,
But we all wait for death
Expecting resurrection
At the hands
Of something more than dramatic overtones,
Bullet wounds,
And bloody dreams.

Silence is underappreciated
When the song is never heard,
Only misunderstood.
You can't expect to be felt
When you're standing on the wrong planet,
Lightyears
From anything they needed.

It's not failure,
It's the surrender of rusty blades
We tasted in the twilight.

I'll write what I must,

I'll refrain from apologies.

If my words are taken personal

It is unintentional;

It's not my responsibility

To lace up a shoe you choose to wear.

THE WEATHER

The weather is changing,
The sky is an exhaled cigarette
Washing away another vacant sunrise.
Lullabies roll from silent lips
As the storm's angry howl
Leaves no doubt
It will break what could never bend.

I defiantly sing songs for a hurricane,
Buried in my stubbornness.
I am nothing more than a road-worn prodigal,
Blistered skin and a ragged heart
Embracing the oncoming devastation.

She is a watermark on a soul
Long given up on
The taste of Alabama moonshine,
The elixir of the night's shifting constellation.
I could follow Orion's belt,
But his sword would sever hope
From my shaking hand;
I am in this until the last note fades
And eyes wither from one more goodbye.

What we want is never free;
Most days the price is too high,
So, we swallow the truth
Like comfort that never comes.
The more I dream of words to heal,
The tighter the blade presses to my throat.

Know you have tasted love

Like a razor of passion on your blooming tongue.

Focus on the afterglow

Trying to fade from your memory;

The flush of skin

Can only hold the darkness at bay for so long.

Let your fingers trace the roadmap

We found in winter's teeth.

THE SHRINE

You have enshrined my love letters,

All the gifts I once gave,

Only to be returned with a hollow goodbye;

You chose to walk out of my life

As if you were merely remaining in character.

My Dear, you deserve an Oscar;

Congratulations on your devastating performance.

I have taken down every picture,

Every keepsake, every silly reminder

I stumble across daily;

I placed them gently in a cardboard box,

Nameless like our love,

Marked only with a broken heart

Sketched on each side.

I have ritualistically removed

Every trace, except one memento

Which whispers your story each night;

Sweet and softly, it sets me off to sleep.

There was always a comfort in your pillow talk,

And I cannot bring myself

To remove it from my bed.

SLIPPING WORDS

Words slip from my mind
A million miles a minute.

I find it difficult to keep up
As my pen furiously scribbles
Random combinations
Until a vague picture begins to form
From the utter chaos.
A final scene, unintended
For anyone other than myself;
Perhaps a way to exorcize
All the damn demons
Tangling in my mind.

I purge these phrases,
Letting the fragments take flight,
Travel the currents of my life,
Get caught in the treetops,
Rustle with the blowing leaves,
Grateful for whoever takes the time
To stumble through
These scattered syllables,
Fragile and creased,
Lying in the mud.

TEXAS MOON

I sail south of Eden

With concertina scars

Like tattoos beneath a west Texas moon.

The horizon, she rages,

Sparklers in the churning clouds,

She's coming in like thunder,

Shaking this barren ground.

Mesmerizing beauty above coyote calls,

Salt sage swaying,

Dancing to rhythm

That demands attention,

The universe is along for the ride.

I'm much too good at tragedy

To see beyond the next funeral pyre;

Give me one hot minute

To burn this tinderbox to ruin.

A thousand miles of ashes now,

The wind just caught its breath;

Going to blow this dream

Through the gates of hell

Before the devil gets a clue.

We're all bound to miss roll call

If we're staring at someone else's shoes.

Don't take my apathy for anger,

Or the love I've got left

For some twisted sort of game.

From where I sit and sat,

No one gets the time they wish for;

We choose the foot we set as balance

And swing our hearts back down our rusty throats.

NAMELESS

We are all
Nameless
Lost photographs,
Forgotten paths.

The story written in our eyes
Tells what cannot be unseen
Unfelt,
And undone.

A portrait
Filled with mistakes,
Mis-strokes,
And mis-opportunities.

We persevere,
Embracing our dark places
While keeping an eye open
For a trace of any coming light.

Some days we need the cold
So warmth is that much warmer;
We need loneliness to create hunger
For more than mediocrity.

Paint your days
In perfect imperfections;
Those will be the moments
Your smile shines the brightest.

HOW FAR IS UP?

We search for something to save us,

To open our ear,

Our hearts,

In a way we have never known;

A soul kiss

In our unraveling.

The cadence of a voice,

The first time

You really heard good jazz,

The way someone's eyes

Stayed locked with yours

While time stood still.

Would it be a fool-hearted thought

That any of these moments

Wouldn't have happened

If you hadn't been ready,

If you hadn't made the effort?

Maybe your subconscious merely

Allowed change to touch your life.

Whether we are ready or not

Our souls know,

And sometimes

Rock bottom

Clears our vision

So we can see

How far up can truly be.

A CARNIVAL OF HEATHENS

Some nights this dark smoky dive bar
Can be a real freak show,
A carnival of heathens.

These are my kind of people,
The ones who have lived their lives,
Busted dreams.

Proud of their broken pieces,
They look for comfort
To walk through the rusty door

And drown out the slow and silent death
Seated at the barstool next to them.
There is always one more barfly.

Ashtrays fill
With cheap lipstick-stained cigarette butts,
The old man at the corner seat

Tells you in minute detail
What a stunner this barfly was,
When she had the world by the tail,

But these days are bottomless tumblers
Filled with the well's finest gin.
Until she breaks a heel

After she powders her nose,
She will slip out the godforsaken door
With her pick of the three widowers

Who have been buying her choice drinks,

Making their arguments

To keep winter away one more night.

Tonight

Might as well be

Love.

ON A DIME

It all stops, turns, changes on a dime;
It's a blink, a breath, a race of time.
We wake in what is left of what we knew
Built up in fault lines and hollow bravado.

No one sees the truth
Behind the facade,
The brand you created
With your own trembling hands;

Filters chosen to accentuate
What you think will catch the eye,
When all you wanted
Was to touch the soul.

And you do;
Every bloodstained word
You scratch out on your own pale skin
Echoes throughout the universe.

But you are too blind
To recognize your own ripple;
You never needed the applause of strangers
Asking for more blood.

Accolades are vaporous in the light of day;
Embrace your gift and believe
The way the few of us can
Who have seen behind the veil.

We have stood in awe your depths;

There is nothing shallow about your art.

This landscape is strewn with half-assed thoughts

Meant to feed empty souls.

You refuse

To condense your soul for anyone,

And there lies your strength;

I hope you see it.

NONARRIVAL

There are times
When you need someone the most
No one arrives,
So you stand shaking
On the cusp of oblivion
Or the discovery of an inner strength
You never imagined possible.

That moment changes everything,
From how you see your day,
How your coffee tastes,
How you feel inside your own skin.
It has been said before:
Rock bottom can recreate you
Or utterly destroy you.

I implore you
Find your resolve,
Create
Who you were born to be:
A beautiful part
Of this unforgiving world.

COLORFUL VOID

A room void of light

Shimmering in shades of blue,

She struts through the doorway

Flaming red,

Unleashing heat from her fire.

Conversation filled with

Too many four-letter adjectives

And predictable innuendos,

Yet she smiles like something amuses her.

I rattle the ice in my glass,

Sip the last few drops greedily,

Never take my eyes off her silhouette.

She perches on the arm of my chair,

Runs her fingers through my hair,

Asks me what I might have planned for the night;

I laugh…she knows damn well

I've never had a plan in my entire life.

Taking her hand

I twirl her around,

Help with her jacket,

Open the door,

Step out into the cool biting night,

Confident this evening

Won't soon be forgotten.

To just let it happen

With no expectations,

We sail down the sparkling pavement,

One with shadows

Destined to live wide awake.

IV. INFINITE

WHAT YOU DON'T KNOW

What you don't know is
The countless brutal hours
She spends alone,
Trying to gather the courage
To face another pointless day.

What you don't know is
How she beats herself up
Over the smallest of things,
Believing she isn't worth the effort.

What you don't know is
This is the three-hundredth consecutive day
She's come home to a cold, empty house
Since the day he passed.

What you don't know
Could be the very reason someone hangs on;
The glimmer of hope
Hung from your casual smile
Passing on a busy sidewalk
A morning she had all but given up.

Be cautious with what you do not know.

REDUCED

I have been reduced to

Sleeping with the lights on.

Your ghost refuses to haunt

Quite so much in illumination,

So I drive out my nighttime shadows

With electric flame.

Sometimes I wake wondering

If I slept at all,

Opening these dry, unfocused eyes,

Spent as the moment I laid my head down;

I suppose no matter how I try,

I can never sweep up the damage you left.

I've slowly been mending,

Perhaps not to the naked eye;

I've been stitching the tears in my heart

With the fragile threads of time,

Sewn loosely with shaking hands,

Numb fingertips.

Maybe I should just invite you back in,

Accept grief as part of who I am now,

Embrace the darkened room,

Let the memory of you

Keep watch over my butchered dreams

While you linger at the foot of this frozen bed.

CAPTIVATED

I am captivated by the sinking moon
Descending as the glow of morning
Begins to blossom.
I have been in heavy thought
Since it first appeared on the horizon,
Watched as it gracefully danced
A solitary line across the heavens,
Filling my heart with longing
For answers I may never learn.
I sometimes think about you
Lying in bed,
Watching the same lunar steps
As it settles on your windowpane
Singing you gentle lullabies
Until your restless mind
Surrenders to the sandman's seduction.
And I can't help but to smile,
Knowing exactly how you sound
As you slip into slumber.
Rest easy, and wake refreshed.

IGNITION

We search
Endless empty spaces
For a taste of anything
That might ignite our souls.
Something warm and wild
Without the aftertaste,
Something real
In a world full of imposters.

You spend fifteen years in the same bed
Buried in a stranger,
To wake one day and understand
This is not the life you chose,
This...is not who you meant to be.
Closets filled with a father's clothes;
Suffocating, dry-cleaned,
Plastic-wrapped suits
Smothered the eyes of the beautiful dreamer
You once were.

GYPSY SMILE

She has gypsy in her smile,
A world in slow-motion
Each time she passes by
With dark eyes
Deeper than a mortal man can survive.

So many have tempted fate
Only to be crushed
On the stones beneath her feet,
Words woven into her hair
Like summer wildflowers
Forever in her heart.

I believe her beauty
Comes from her blindness;
Oblivious to her own natural charms,
Power comes from soft hands,
Gentle lips speak velvet healing,
Warmth keeps winter's pain away.

BLACK POWDER

She's loading up on black powder

And digging shrapnel out of the walls.

Prepare yourself for a fight.

A battle.

A war.

She will set up barricades,

Then cut you down where you stand.

Once the air raid siren sounds off

There is no surrender,

Merely a chance to die with dignity.

If you believe you were the first

To be laid to waste, you are a fool;

Accept your fate

As the verbal bullets fly,

Embrace this glorious ending.

You may one day

Return to the living

A ghost, perhaps

Haunting old battlefields.

The smell of sulfur and cold memories

Will hang heavy in the stale air.

You'll want to forget it all;

Instead, you'll remain a museum

Of yesterday's loss.

THE CURATOR

Being caretaker of the museum
Of my heart isn't always easy. Seems

There is always a mess to clean.
So many exhibits at varied stages
Of disrepair, the upkeep has finally
Become more of a burden than I can

Bear. I can no longer afford to keep
The lights on; all the portraits of

Your smile faded. The abstract
Structures in remembrance of what
We once had now collapse,
Returning to the dust which made

Them. The centerpiece our
Sculpted hearts intertwined, now
Cracked, crumbling, and appearing
More a pile of rubble than the

Love they were supposed to represent. If
It's time to set these tapestries aflame,
Lock the doors and finish the
Job you started without a goodbye.

There is nothing left here for me.

DELICATE

Delicate to the eye,

She draws you in

To admire the way the sunlight

Glows on her petals

Grounded in the soil,

Wrapped around

Thoughts of bedrock in her veins,

Stronger than anyone sees on the surface.

The earth will shake and crumble,

Yet she will continue to bloom,

Knowing nothing

Can erase her mark on the world.

In electric dreams,

She chases what is already hers,

Happiness will follow in the letting go,

Settling into the here and now

While yesterday burns to ash.

A fresh pen

To write between the lines

And along the margins.

Feathers and needles,

Birds of prey,

Birds of song

Waking in the blushing dawn,

Soul exposed to cold hands and broken hearts.

You are chosen to be

The place she rests her head and her bones,

Tired of a lifetime

Filled with stones cast into the ocean,

Wishes washed away in the ebbing tide.

The taste of bruised tenderness,

Bitten in restless exhaustion,

The jealous moon hides

Behind darkening, silver-lined clouds.

Breathe in the fragrance,

Heather and wildwood

Linger on pulsing skin.

She sits quietly in the valley of time

Waiting to be a painting

In the halls of your chest, priceless.

THE GREEN VELVET CHAIR

You sit in that green velvet chair,

Streetlight slips through the window,

Falls across your right eye,

Illuminated.

Seated before me,

Memories of childhood dreams

Dance in the colors of your eye.

I am suspended;

You are somewhere else

Absentmindedly tracing the rim of your glass.

The first drink went down smooth,

A much-needed shock to the system,

A calming of the inner storm.

Replaying all the times you died,

All the mornings you awoke

In the ashes of bonfires from the night before.

Skin aflame with kisses,

Handprints tattooed upon you

Never to be washed away.

And you stare out into the darkening street,

Your pupil widens,

Movies roll inside your head.

We all die

A thousand times;

That is the sum of life.

I watch you return to the now;

A slight smile,

A slow blink.

Turning your head my way,

You raise the tumbler to your lips,

Leave a perfect lipstick print on the glass.

Condensation drips,

The lucid skin of your breast

Glistens.

The drop travels down,

Disappearing

Under your blouse.

You never flinch,

You simply look over your almost empty drink,

The corner of your mouth curves.

You can see the desire;

My ardent gaze, your glow;

Our moments entwine.

Enraptured in the twilight,

Perhaps you have been replaying

Our every candlelit scene.

All I know is

You are

The most beautiful part of my life.

The beat of this soul

Is safely enfolded inside that chest,

And I never want it back.

This is where my story ends;

Your hands,

My heart.

Your lungs

Breathing me in,

No exhale.

Breathlessly into forever,

We sit face to face,

Exchanging bourbon kisses.

Offering me your glass, you whisper,

It's time to leave,

Loverboy,

This love is overdue.

DISHEVELED

I am disheveled,
Somewhere between disarray
And wreckage.
I lean over the sink,
Hands on the vanity,
Looking at the mess of my reflection.

Where the hell have I been?
How did I end up here?
I wet my hair,
Splash water on my face,
Hope when I open my eyes
I'll see the person
I remember myself to be.

But the ragged soul remains,
A vacant stare,
Slight confusion
Behind my sleepless eyes.
The voice inside reminds me,
You have lost a decade
With nothing to show for it.

I exhale
Through the drops of water on my lips;
I refuse to lose another ten years
Trying to recapture
What has been washed away
Down the river of time.

I choose to make a mark

With the days I have left;

It is never too late to finish strong.

QUIET RAGE

All the years of quiet rage
Made the halls of my heart
Like patchwork;
Self-inflicted punches
Left holes in my mind.

I swallowed my anger,
Hiding the roots of my fear.

Fear of not being enough,
Not seeing any worth
In who I am,
Who I was,
Who I could be.

As time passes
I still walk these halls.

In the war zone where I lived
All inside my head,
I have come to accept myself,
All my flaws,
All my weaknesses.

I hold flowers in the hand
That once dealt quiet rage.

THUNDERHEAD

A storm rustles

On the horizon,

Splinters of lightning

From a belly of clouds.

I stand weathered,

Ready for a hurricane,

Refusing to wither,

Denying the breaking.

The whispers of severing

Flesh from bone

Heal in the bleeding

Head full of bruises,

Mouth full of rain.

Tell me what I need

And look behind the veil,

Tattered like love songs

Swept out to sea.

Unworthily grateful,

I always find

Everything is temporary

Except for this stain

Of you and me

And our last dying breath.

SILENTLY

I silently watch her read
Her favorite Whitman passages;
Morning light illuminates her skin
Like a thousand candles
In a world of darkness.

She sips her sweet coffee
From an oversized mug,
Eyes never leaving the page;
She is stunning, effortlessly mesmerizing,
A goddess among mortal men.

I am content to share the same space,
Smiling from knowing
Beauty can still be found
Behind books in coffee shops.

SATELLITE

Keep your eyes on the sky.

She'll be coming back around;

She's a satellite

Counting constellations

Before she burns out in the afterglow

Wide awake, yet dreaming

Of how this ground holds no comfort

Like the arms of a stranger,

Tumblers of golden poison

Stain lips of reverie.

She leaves no judgment

Lingering languid in rustling sheets;

It is bitten fruit,

Sweet and salty, untethered

In the way she paints this moment in time,

Fractures of a tock

Silent in the breathing skipped tick

As she slips into your veins,

Wakes you in a fevered dream.

Toes in the river

She calls your name,

The unraveling,

The spiral inwards

So familiar;

Rescued from what you learned

To hate about yourself

The birth of a miracle.

Eyelids heavy from the sedating siren's wail,

We were alive for a moment,

Yet were lost from the beginning;

No sense denying the obvious,

Ruins hide the bones of yesterday's lives.

Here we sit,

Sun bleached beneath a stone archway;

Not all satellites sell sanctuary.

FORGOTTEN WORDS

We forget words

Like *love, lust,* and *bitten skin;*

No one answers our plea for remedy,

No one cures this illness.

Us and the angels

Set fire to the wilderness;

Our banner year

Becomes fodder for the frontline.

We rail against these changes,

Yet it brings the new point of view we need;

I stall,

My soul's fabric altered.

I have to believe

Certain vocal harmonies

Are the rapture incarnate;

They reach the part of me

That's been hanging onto its last breath for decades;

Now caught up in the anointing,

I realize I haven't been alive for years.

What do we do with an angel's breath

And a heart full of catacombs?

Set the ruins free to circle the moon

Or throw another *could've been* on the pyre?

Spellbound in the sparrow's song,

She knows how to draw me in,

Knows how to break my heart,

Fevered and frayed,

Punctured with yesterday's errant arrow;

A cherub with an axe to grind

Splits hairs over coffee stains and old sweaters,

Entitled to the reverie,

But blistered in the echo's refrain.

THE WALLFLOWER

She believes herself a wallflower
As each partner passes
Never slowing their pace,
But those eyes are dark and endless
Like the taste of a warm fall,
Those lips are made for passion
To speak in angels' tongues.

The spark of the universe,
She lingers inside my head
Smiling politely, her hunger
Hidden from blind hearts.

She dreams of more than beige days,
Her strength colorful like her fingernails;
She is a Christmas morning
For the one lucky enough
To unwrap her boundless heart.
Put your ear to her beating chest,
Embrace a healing world of honeyed kisses.

She will resurrect your battered soul.

WAITING WISHES

We wait to be wishes

Soaking in sunlight,

Our fragile bones

Anticipating liftoff,

Catching a gentle breath

That might carry us

Where we were meant to root.

We grow between the blades

Through the rocky soil against every odd,

We blossom

Beautiful in the right pair of eyes.

A universe at the foot of everything

We were afraid to ask or speak aloud,

Do we dare open our bloom

To the thunder in their voice?

Hoping for rain,

Expecting hail,

The reckoning of sins

Left on tangled tongues.

Our past has barbs;

The weight heavy most days,

Eliciting a shutdown.

As much as we fight the fleeing,

We must push through the conditioning

And inevitably run.

We begin by forgiving ourselves

For the fool we played

Many lifetimes over;

How we try to braid the loose ends

Of our fraying hearts.

Losses like shallow veins

Beneath rice paper thin skin,

Life is lived between *hallelujahs*.

We cling to sweet resurrections

Like spent lovers

Wrapped in the afterglow of dawn,

Fresh as newborn eyes.

Hearts race

With unspoken gratitude,

Prayers of Babylon

Songs of undeserved redemption

Soak into the ether,

Salvation bathes

In the coming storm.

THE DREAMCATCHER

The dreamcatcher appeared to be empty as I removed it from the window. The feathers fluttered in the rising breeze and I left the window open so anything caught would have a second chance somewhere outside my room. It is a solemn moment when you are about to see all the bad dreams you've been spared. Most of us live through heartache and pain hoping one day there won't be any more loss of sleep or loss of hope.

I held the dreamcatcher in my hands and shook until I saw confetti hearts, stardust, and forgotten prayers. We burn in the moonlight—a splintered hallelujah stillborn in time. The air heavy with finality, resolute in unanswered choices, blind spots, and a bloody nose. Names remain forgotten out of self-preservation, but tattoos remain. As much as I hope the catcher will be thorough, I still find beach sand and stray hairs littering my thoughts and sheets, sticky webs strung between a gateway to the subconscious.

We have the chance to run from realities we didn't choose and destinations we could never afford, but were more or less everything we needed whether wanted them or not.

My train of thought stalls in the morning light and I am left with tears on my face, mourning for lost love, wish-less stars, and foreign tongues that once spoke a sacred name in the darkness. She was never mine to hold and I was always spinning out of orbit, brittle in the way *I love you* always broke the silence like a gunshot. We aren't always ready for the way it ricochets off breastplates and heartbeats like a song we can't shake off our skin.

We find ourselves dancing like falling rain

Or the debris lost in the dreamcatcher

Left in my open window.

FOR MY GRANDSON

I believe in you;

You are the future

And you will make a difference.

I found a book and immediately thought of you

Giving it to your grandchild one day

When I'm merely a faded memory of better times

And you fly until you fall into my arms again.

I will be watching,

Smiling from wherever it is I land

After my final exhale,

Scattered on the wind like the dust I came from.

We are cut from the same piece of leather,

Souls weathered throughout lifetimes

Until we crossed paths.

Now it is my responsibility to let you know

You are never alone;

I am a thought away from you

Eternally.

Believe in yourself,

The great things you can accomplish

With drive, resilience, and perseverance.

I just want you to know

I love you,

My little cub.

I always will.

DIVIDING LINES

We see the line

Between where we grind our lives away

And where we end up

The shell of who we are,

So we give away our gold

In exchange for a stone

That tells no story

Of the dash between the dates.

We must own our responsibility

And burn through the red ink,

Building a storyline

About how we held fire in our mouths

Illuminating our lover's veins

With an adrenaline rush, bruising thighs.

Sky bolden,

Rainy gray glow

Feeds the turning world,

Burns, no filter needed,

Slips silently into the expanding daylight,

Swallows spring

As the equinox fades

And the solstice approaches.

We hope time suspends

In the apex of summer's sweat,

And the pendulum reverses its path

Into the dimming twilight,

Wearing moonlight

Like a promise ring.

CAUTIOUS REFRAIN

Fading memories

Grow in the lengthening darkness,

Bruises cause the night sky to shimmer

A hopeful recovery, yet cautious refrain.

When the roses wilt,

The last fragrance of love lingers,

Those faded blooms

A last note from a forgotten serenade.

We stand in shadows

Clutching charms

From tarnished silver strings,

Broken latches,

And busted locks with rusted keys;

Freedom is buried

In the heart of a bad dream.

FIND A WAY

Do they love you the way I should have?

How you needed me to,

How you deserved me to?

Do they worship at your altar with celestial tongue

Breathing a hallelujah into your confessional?

I admit I was lost in the fabric of life,

A fallen heart in the seams of living

With darkness as a road map,

Trusting faith would guide me home.

Oddly, it never did.

I am still here shaken to my roots,

A silhouette against a sunset,

A sleeping tree ornamented in a murder,

Skies filled with black-winged symphonies

Awaiting their time to perch.

A witness to the undoing,

Love is beauty bathed in blood;

We are never clean

From that first arrow

Piercing the chambers of our heart.

Own the barbs,

A rose's thorns bring rapture

Meant for sunlight and rain,

Swallow their shine, and accept

What was meant to be will find a way.

OPTIMISTIC AND SUBTLE

When he was young, he had no idea
How dark a storm could rage,
How Life's rain can snuff a dream
Optimistic and subtle as concertina wire
Lit up like an Indian summer.

He believed mountains were part of the path,
Pushed forward relentless as a fevered lover;
Perhaps it was a bit naive
To keep believing the best
Through the heartbreaks, the scars, the wreckage.

He couldn't give in to the pain he swallowed,
Wouldn't change course for simpler roads;
It was the undoing that forged his strength for tomorrow,
Opened his eyes to more kindness
And less judgement.

He hung from a precipice
Scared as hell,
Yet he knew
In the falling
Would be a chance to fly.

He never knew where he might land,
But he had faith
It would be in the proper direction;
In the moving forward
He would find himself among the living.

Trying to raise the dead before they are lost forever

Begins with a step in any direction

Away from stagnation.

Believe, pursue, grow;

Life will finally feel like you lived it.

HEART OF GLASS

Thought I was in love, it was a gas;
Soon found out
Deborah Harry's chime
Masked a heart of glass.

The first taste of love
Exhilarating,
We feel immortal,
A sense that anything is attainable.

Such raw power
Rewires our synapses
With a steady drip of serotonin

...Before the fallout.

Then comes a series of second guesses,
Second chances, and seconds lost;
No matter how we rewrite the equation,
We end up shattered.

Do we learn from our fracturing
Or continue blindly
Chipping away
At fragile artifacts?

This delicate vessel
Is resilient,
A veteran of every battle
With no hesitation.

Your heart knows the secret of life

Is finding your feet again

Though the fleeting moments

Be golden.

And if we live to die a thousand times

Remember,

We escaped hell

A thousand and one.

HOPE

The difference
Between crumbling
And holding on,

The distance from
Giving up
To giving more,

From sundown
To sunrise,

Between accepting it is over
To believing
There's still a chance:

A four-letter word
Etched into the dash
Between the dates

Hope

CRUEL CLOSURE

The story ends,
No fond farewells.

Some narratives
Hang like an old shirt
in the back of the closet

You never
Were brave enough
To clean out.

This is not how
You pictured
The last page;

Things should've
Been said.

How a slow burn
Can fade into
A starless night...

Now you wrestle with
The cold ghost
Of cruel closure.

Acknowledgements

When I began writing to purge my headaches and heartaches, I had no idea where it would lead. I have wrestled my mind from precarious ledges my whole life and always found solace in the way words embraced me over and over, showing me there is always a glow behind the grey.

On this journey, I have met some beautiful souls who have continued to inspire me daily with a kind word or a gentle touch. I count myself an extremely blessed man with the friends I have made over the years, and to each of them I want to say thank you for being both the push and safety net I needed to press forward towards dreams I never knew were attainable. Life will only get better and brighter no matter how dark the storm is that rages around me.

To my family and friends, thank you for believing in me even when I struggled to find a grain of faith to believe anything was worth sharing. What an amazing group of people I have grown to call friends.

Much love to you all. Thank you.

ABOUT THE AUTHOR

Thomas Hinds is a father of three. He has spent the last several years as a troubadour, traveling across the country playing both his own songs, as well as tunes that shaped his personal style. He first released *In The Details*, which was his first book of poetry and prose, in 2020. For this second edition, he has reworked the collection, as well as added several new pieces. This collection showcases his flair for painting a scene with his words, as well as his individualized approach to expressing the laments we all have in common. Whether loss or love, tragedy or triumph, Thomas brings you into the life he has lived.

He spent his formative years in central Wyoming before moving to northwest New Mexico with his mother and sister. Spending his youth in jagged, wide-open spaces, shaped Thomas's point of view and helped him see the world through the eyes of a dissonant landscape. This still influences his unique perspective.

In addition to his poetry, Thomas is also an accomplished songwriter. He has released two full length albums, *Ghosts and Lamentations* (2015) and *Resurrection Road* (2019), as well as an EP titled *Barbwire Bouquet* (2017)—a single release of his song "Luminous" (2020), and *Heart Attacks & Sweet Dreams* (2022), a six song EP. He also recently released a third full-length album, *Where Do We Go From Here* (2023).

Thomas stays busy playing on the road, working on his next collection of prose, as well as a follow up album to *Where Do We Go From Here*.

You can find more info on Thomas and his work at
www.thomashindsmedia.com.

Please leave a review for any of Thomas's material, and he will see you
out on the road.

"In the end, scars are proof of life."
Thomas Hinds